HELP!

WHAT TO DO WHEN YOUR SMALL BUSINESS NEEDS AN EMPLOYEE

BY

LYN RICHARDS

This book is a work of non-fiction. Names of people and places have been changed to protect their privacy.

First published by AuthorHouse 05/11/04

ISBN: 1-4184-5981-X (e-book)
ISBN: 1-4184-3660-7 (Paperback)

Printed in the United States of America
Bloomington, IN

This book is printed on acid free paper.

INTRODUCTION

I have been a Certified Public Accountant working with small business owners for over 20 years. Over the years, the most common complaint I've heard is that it is *just impossible to find good help.* Indeed, as a small business owner myself, I've said the same thing.

Michael Gerber, in his book *The E-Myth Revisited,* outlines some of the reasons most small business owners start their businesses. There is the entrepreneur who truly believes they've got a unique offering and can fill a niche in the market that no one else can. Or they feel they can make more money, have more independence, and do things the "right way" by going into business for themselves. Sometimes, they start a business to build something. They intend to have a family legacy, or an asset to sell upon retirement. They **never** start their business with the goal of becoming an employer! And yet, no other skill will serve them better in building a business that remains competitive in the market, delivers a consistent product, and is an independent asset useful for selling or passing on to heirs.

The E-Myth Revisited tells the story of a pie maker who goes through the usual nightmare of hiring help. Either the employee fails to deliver the services or product exactly like the owner wishes, or the opposite is true: the employee becomes invaluable, then quits. And that is exactly what I see everyday in my practice. For every small business owner I serve, I feel like I'm waiting for that shoe to drop. The business owner either has an overpaid employee that is under-functioning, or has an employee that they are over-reliant upon who may quit. Either way, the owner is faced with the constant stress of knowing that on any day, at any time, his (already too heavy) work load may double as a result of employee transition.

When that shoe finally does drop the owner often gives up and goes back to doing it all himself. They try to make do without replacing the worker, intentionally limiting growth and expansion. They're putting themselves at risk since their business depends exclusively on them. If they're suddenly unable to work, the business will fail. At the minimum, they are working too hard for not enough money, thus running a higher risk of burnout. Sometimes they restructure the job to be less challenging and lower paid. They think this means they'll have an easier time trying to fill the position and they'll be less hurt when the employee leaves. Or they devise "incentives" to boost productivity or loyalty. Most often these are just several complicated hoops for the employee to jump in order to get paid decently. These "incentives" rarely inspire productivity or loyalty though.

Since the most common question I get from my clients is "How do I find someone to work for me?" I've spent some time and money on researching the response. This book is offered as a step-by-step solution to equip small business owners to be successful employers. The book is organized by first addressing some popular myths about human resources, and then provides specific steps to find the right person for the job. The steps work regardless of the size of the business, whether one employee or a hundred. It is written in a language that small business owners will understand. The book is designed to help the business become a place that runs like clockwork, where employees are competent, loyal, and happy in the workplace. Following these guidelines will help the owner maximize the business's largest monetary investment, the team.

There are additional resources and some general guidelines about how to manage payroll at the end of the book.

I suggest using the book as a workbook. Do one chapter at a time. Make some notes as you go along, writing down what you think of as you go. Then stop reading and follow the specific idea of the chapter. Start reading again after you've completed that task.

If you read the whole book at one time, the process may become overwhelming for someone new at hiring. Taking one chapter at a time will help you manage each step in small increments and boost the chances for your success in becoming an employer.

In writing this I owe a huge debt of gratitude to RanOne, the leading global network of accountants devoted to delivering resources to those of us who serve small business owners, for their resources and guidance in my own human resource journey.

TABLE OF CONTENTS

CHAPTER I – RETHINKING CERTAIN MYTHS

Let's start by rethinking some traditional employment myths. There are four that make me cringe when I hear my small business client owners verbalizing them. Here they are and the reasons they should be exposed as myths.

"They should count themselves lucky to have a job". In the Great Depression, this was true! Folks *were* lucky to have a job! However, at the time of this writing, unemployment is not as rampant. There will always be a certain percentage of the work force that is unemployed due to corporate restructures, moves and relocations, or family changes. When unemployment percentages are in the single digits, there is virtually no unemployment. Even if America would suddenly slump into double-digit unemployment, it would take some time before people really feel desperate to find *any* sort of job.

The reality of today's market place is the prevailing attitude that everyone deserves a job. Notice I said they deserve a job. Jobs are widely regarded as the right of every able-bodied worker. While some employees take this attitude to the extreme, my point is that you are unlikely to find anyone to work in your business who feels lucky just to have a job.

When a small business owner has the idea that his employees are lucky to have a job, any job, they communicate disrespect for the employee and limited appreciation. They are laying the groundwork in their business for high employee turnover, because most people won't work in this type of atmosphere in today's society.

"They'll never find a better place to work than this". Not true! Even if it were true, human nature is such that they will certainly find grass that *looks* greener! Every business will have employees who decide to leave for a "better offer". More on how to deal with this is in the last chapter.

One reason this is a myth is that every employer needs to be constantly changing the workplace. Nothing in life is constant except change. Believing this means that you realize that a workplace can always be improved.

The downside to allowing yourself to think this way is that you'll be blind-sided when your team members leave you for a better offer. The best way to think about your work place is to know that you've done your best in what you offer, and that there will be someone, somewhere, who will appreciate your place of business as a working environment.

"There are no good employees out there". Another version of this myth is "folks just don't want to work anymore", or "this younger generation is so spoiled". Again, while there are examples of folks who do fit this mold, most people will enjoy an honest day's work for a fair wage.

One reason this myth exists is that small business owners hire folks and assume they'll know what to do. They think the job should be common sense. But this disregards the respect your employee may have for doing things the way you want them done. The reality is that people like to work independently, they like to work knowing what is expected of them, and they like to have a sense of completion about the job they do. Provide them with the tools to work independently, get the job done, and done the way you expect them to do it and you should have a happy, productive worker. Following the steps outlined in this book will greatly enhance your potential for someone to work in your place of business.

The truth is that unspoken expectations are what lead employers to believe that their work force is slack. Failure to clearly communicate the job leads to a poor performance, a frustrated employee and employer, and high turnover.

"They are staff, I am a professional". This speaks to a class-minded employer who will be perceived as having a superior attitude. No one likes to feel like a second class citizen.

Try to adopt the phrases "team member" and "associate" or "colleague". These make your employee feel more like an essential part of your product or service, rather than the proletariat. Treating your team with respect will bring respect for you, and lower your turnover cost.

The cost of turnover is extremely high. There are a number of theories on what the actual cost is. You can find a worksheet on the web to try to put numbers to it. While this is a good start, it won't capture all the intangible costs to turnover. Turnover costs not only dollars, but time, efficiency, office moral, and customer perception of your work place. When your customers see a revolving door of team members, it sows a seed of doubt in their minds as to how good you really are. The cost of all of this is really difficult to qualify. Rethinking some of theses myths will help get you started on the right track to minimizing team turnover.

CHAPTER II – THE OVERRIDING MANTRA

The first and most important rule of human resource management is

HIRE ATTITUDE, TRAIN COMPENTENCE.

When hiring someone, your business will reap benefit more from a team member with a "can do" attitude and no experience, than one with a bad attitude and twenty years experience. If you follow the steps in this book, hiring someone with a good attitude will result in that employee developing into a competent employee. You can never train attitude. If it's lacking from the get-go, it will always be lacking.

Hire someone willing to take orders. Although you may feel that you need someone to work independently, this is not the same as someone who is willing to take orders. Working independently is common to most all personality types, taking orders is not. In order for you to be confident that your products and services are being consistently delivered in the manner you specify, you'll need to have a person willing to do it your way. This is a tough skill to interview for, but asking the right questions can help you determine if you're getting this right.

Find a team member who is interested puzzles. This is a tremendous attribute. There is a certain personality type that enjoys figuring out how to get solutions, and that is a valuable trait in an employee. This is especially important if your business is in its infancy stages, where a good team member can offer a fresh eye with regard to efficiency and process. It also means that they'll find a way to solve a unique situation when you're not available. When you interview, ask if solving cross-word puzzles or jigsaw puzzles is one of their hobbies.

Ask them what their long term goals are. Even if the goals are not related to your business, find someone with ambition. They're more likely to be eager to learn new things, and more likely to offer expansion resources to your business. One way to discover this is by looking at a resume. A resume with a broad range of experience (notice I said "experience" not "jobs") in a short time shows a person who is willing and eager to learn new things.

Avoid folks who are averse to change. These are the employees who will want to do the same thing, over and over, for an indefinite period of time. These folks are better suited to a large business where systems are really set. A small business requires fluid and dynamic change. Flexibility is a key attribute for your team.

A pleasant demeanor is critical. People who smile and greet you warmly will make your workplace a more pleasant place to work, thus boosting productivity and morale. Customer service is critical to the success of any small business. And in any small business, almost every member of your team will have customer contact. So hire someone nice.

I realize that it may not be possible to find a person with all these wonderful attributes. Select the ones that are most important to you and look for them when you're interviewing.

Remember that this chapter opens by emphasizing attitude over experience. So what could be wrong with hiring experience? Here are a few thoughts.

A frequent mistake I see is an employer who hires someone with experience in order to avoid taking the time to train. The "no train" employee is a myth, no matter their experience. Let's face it, if your business did things exactly the same as one of your competitors, there would be no reason for you to be on your own! So that's the very least of what you'll do to train someone – teach them how YOU want things done. And that's bound to be different than the way they've been doing things.

When you see that training is critical you can see that people who don't want to be trained are trouble. If you've advertised for experience, and perhaps even communicated that you don't want to spend a lot of time training someone, you're attracting the wrong sort of folks; those who are averse to training.

A person who is being selected for their experience is being given the distinct impression that their experience is valuable (which it very well may be). But this may lead your new hire to believe that their input on how things should be done is invaluable. This can become extreme. Before you know it, you're being questioned about your competence. This is your business, and you don't need anyone else to help you run it!

Hiring someone based upon what they've done in the past leads them to think that you want things done the way they've always done them. And you may get some argument if you want to do things differently.

Lastly, ask yourself why a person with vast experience is looking for a new job. This requires more careful consideration than hiring for attitude. An employee with years of experience, a great attitude, and a willing spirit is invaluable. Why has their current employer allowed them to be discontent to the point of seeking employment elsewhere? It is more likely that the employee has become disgruntled about something. Be careful that you know what it is that has caused the employee to seek a new position doing the same thing!

Of course, bad attitudes in general don't even warrant discussion. Terminate the interview or the employee immediately.

Of course, if you can find both attitude and competence, you've really hit the jackpot. This is rare, but it can be done.

Relocations due to spousal transfers, family issues, or prior business difficulties can turn up some real gems for potential new team members. This means it's a good idea to find out why they are interested in switching jobs during the interview.

When forced to choose, remember:

HIRE ATTITUDE, TRAIN COMPETENCE

CHAPTER III – ASSESS (OR RE-ASSESS) THE ORGANIZATIONAL CHART OF YOUR COMPANY.

One of the ideas put forth in *The E-Myth Revisited*, by Michael Gerber, is the importance of an organization chart for your business. Here is the basic model:

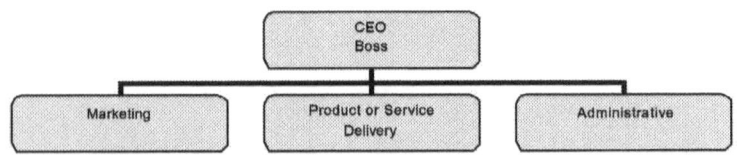

It is important to start with this model as it is (read: do not think that there can ever be more than one boss). There are always three divisions to any business. Beyond that, the chart can be tailored according to your particular business. For example, your business might be carpet cleaning. In this case, you would have a lot of organizational sub-titles and headings under product or service delivery, but not so much under administration. A business that is totally service oriented may not have much marketing because business might be primarily by referral.

One boss is critical. Never hire someone and give them a big "say so" immediately. Never hire someone who's looking for "say so"! Your business needs a leader, and only one of them. Of course, after time, you'll want to include team members in decision making to help them buy into decisions and resulting policies. But only one boss should ever have the final authority, and this should always be clear.

For a very small business, your name might be in every box! That is OK. The chart is still useful. It can give you an idea about budgeting your time and the direction you want to move in next.

Once you've put yourself in the chart, go ahead and add personnel. If you don't have many the people now, just put in something like "new hire". In fact, to make the chart more long-range, put in folks you intend to hire way down the road. While you're adding the people to the chart, think about the slot they'll be filling.

Start by thinking about what will grow your business in the best manner. Often business owners hire someone to do the things they absolutely hate to do. This may not be in the best interest of the business. Just because you don't like taking the trash out, don't assign it to a new team member if you need them to be out of the office doing sales calls. Your business is separate from you, it has its own needs, and those may be different than yours.

By the same token, be open to changing your job responsibilities. For example, if you've never administered payroll, you'll have to start doing it now! This will add hours to your week, making it possible that you'll want to move some of your other duties to the new hire.

One thing I see fairly often is the small business owner wanting a sales person as their first or second new hire. But this is not always the best idea. Before bringing more sales in the door you need to have the systems in place to deliver the product consistently and accurately. If you don't, you may be bringing in new customers that may leave dissatisfied, and defeat effective marketing. So, in deciding which base to cover in a new hire, try to think of the chain of events that will happen from the moment the customer decides to buy from you to the payment upon completion, and make sure all the links are in place. Look at your organization chart. If you have a big huge "sales" box, and little teeny "administrative" and "products/services" box, the chart quickly becomes disproportionate. My experience is that it is better to have your organization running smoothly, consistently and efficiently, and with excess capacity, before you hire a sales person.

CHAPTER IV – WRITE UP A JOB DESCRIPTION AND CALCULATE THE COST.

Using the work you did in the previous chapter, set about writing a detailed job description. Be *very* detailed. For example, don't just write down "answer the phone". Write down how you want it answered. Do you want people to say "good morning"? How about giving their name? Do you want them to screen your calls? What type of message do you want them to take? Do you want them to say "you'll need to call back later"? Do you want them to always write down the phone number of the caller so you'll have it at your fingertips for returning the call? This is the kind of detail you need in advance of interviewing people. It saves so much training time later, and it makes the job crystal clear for a candidate.

Try to keep the boxes in your organization chart separate when writing up job descriptions. Realizing that in a small business this may not always be possible, it is still a good idea to structure the job to stay in one area of the business. This avoids a team member feeling like they are covering too many bases and becoming overwhelmed. Also, it avoids (real or perceived) over-reliance upon any one employee. If you are a brand new employer you might be hiring someone to cover more than one area. But keeping the "boxes separate" at this stage will position you for growth when that job becomes too big for one person. Be honest with your new hire that you are asking them to cover both jobs because the business is in a growth phase. This may actually have the effect of exciting them about working with a growing business, as it presents different opportunities for them.

You might want to refer to the mission statement of your business when writing up job descriptions. It will ensure that you don't forget vital customer service information. You may also get additional ideas of things that you've wanted to implement, but haven't had the time or the personnel to put in place.

As part of the big picture, keep this written job description as part of your business's operations manual. It's a great way to start an Operations Manual if you haven't already.

The next step is to carefully calculate the cost of a new hire. There's a fair amount of work involved in this to do it properly. Start by researching salary ranges. You can do this on the internet by searching the category "benchmarking salaries" or "human resources". There are a variety of resources under these topics and many are free. You may also have a local professional organization that can help you learn what similar positions are paid at in your area. Try contacting your local Chamber of Commerce, they generally are a resource. And, if you are comfortable with it, ask your competitors if they'll tell you what they pay folks.

Once you have a base salary in mind, add fringes. At the minimum, fringes are the social security taxes (7.65% of the gross, up to over $90,000) and unemployment taxes (about 3.5% of the first $7,000 in wages). Generally if you have more than three employees, you'll need a workers' compensation insurance policy. This premium is based upon wages; it varies from state to state and by the nature of the job. Your insurance broker can help you with this. Other fringes would include health insurance, cafeteria plans, and retirement.

Next, add the cost of providing the worker with the resources to be able to do their job. This might include a phone line, a desk, day timer, a cell phone, a small quantity of office supplies, uniforms and auto expenses. There's no point in hiring someone new if you don't give them the proper tools to do the job. By estimating what this will cost you avoid feeling overwhelmed by dollars *after* you've hired someone. And you build the new relationship based upon your generosity and respect for what you expect the employee to do.

There is a worksheet at the back of this book that can help you calculate the cost. See Chapter XIV, the second resource.

One final word, often small businesses try to avoid the nightmare of employment tax compliance and payroll tax expense by paying people either "under the table" or as an independent contractor. No question, payroll is no fun. However, "under the table" is not a part of the tax code that exempts the payments from being tax fraud. In other words, it is a felony. Paying folks as an independent contractor may serve you well in the short term, but in the long run it rarely works. In the event of an audit, the IRS will likely determine the person to be an employee, subjecting your business to penalties. If, in fact, they are an independent contractor, they will be liable for all social security taxes plus income tax on whatever you report to the IRS at the end of the calendar year. This requires the individual to make estimated tax payments. Very frequently, they don't make the payments. In about eighteen months their tax debt is overwhelming and the IRS has located them for withholding. They usually quit at this point, and move on to either avoid the IRS hounding them for payment or to get a job that will withhold the taxes on a regular basis. Then you've incurred turnover cost instead of payroll tax cost. When you enter the world of being an employer, just bite the bullet and absorb the cost of proper compliance. There are a few resources in plain language at the end of the chapter. Contact your accountant for help with properly setting it up, and be sure you understand your responsibilities as an employer.

If you really think you have someone that qualifies as an independent contractor, there is a 21 point test that you can take on the IRS website at www.irs.gov.

CHAPTER V – ADVERTISING THE JOB

The next thing to tackle in finding a team member is to solicit the job. There are a few mediums to use, but the tone should be the same regardless of the medium you choose.

Employment agencies are widely used in some areas. Years ago on the west coast, the most qualified candidates and the elite employers used these agencies. It was perceived that the most qualified employees would be selective about a potential job. The employer who used one of these agencies was charged a fairly substantial fee. The employer then had the benefit of applicants who were screened, and possibly tested, by the agency. The employee knew that he would be referred to a company that was willing to invest in him. However, in South Carolina these agencies are not as widely used. In fact, my experience with them is their offerings can be people who are having difficulty finding permanent employment. The pool of applicants tends to be less qualified and less experienced. Employers here tend not to use the agencies for permanent positions, and rely instead on word-of-mouth or newspaper advertising. So it depends on your prevailing local customs as to whether it is a good idea to use an agency or not.

Regardless of whether you use an agency or not, the job must be advertised. How you advertise it will determine the response you get.

Start by thinking about why someone would want to come to work in your business. What is it that you like about your products or services? What is it that is valuable to your customers? Think about what you like about your work environment. This should be the content of your advertisement.

Starting by listing all the tasks in detail that you expect will only bore a potential respondent. Also, it makes the job appear slavish and no fun! The person you are looking for will have a sense of enthusiasm and eagerness in the form of their attitude. Listing the tasks in the ad doesn't attract the attitude you'll need.

Advertise in more than one section of the newspaper. For example you might want to advertise for an administrative assistant in both the office section and the administrative section. Think outside of the box. You might get a response from someone eager to learn new things, someone who is looking for a new challenge. Also, choose the paper you advertise in by its readership. An accounting firm is not likely to get a response from the local *Free Times*, but I have a veterinarian client who gets wonderful response from *Free Times* ads.

The tone of the advertisement will determine the type of person that applies. I recently placed an ad asking for "a vibrant, vital team member who wants to work in a congenial office". I got just that, vibrant resumes that were creative, informative and congenial. It laid the ground work for me to interview a lot of candidates with the right attitudes.

Try to avoid putting the salary in the advertisement. If you must, put a salary range. If you advertise too low, you may lose a good prospect. If you advertise too high, you'll be flooded with extra work in sifting through volumes of resumes.

Ask for a response either in the form of a fax or a blind email box. The regular mail adds another couple of days to the response. A P.O. Box is very impersonal and requires a trip to the Post Office to pick up the responses. Your work address is too much information; you'll have unwanted interruptions with people dropping by. Also, a phone number for a fax is shorter, thus cutting the cost of the advertisement.

When you get your responses, wait about three days before doing any screening. Some of the resumes will be so awful that you'll throw them away immediately. These would include lots of grammatical and spelling errors, very little education, or an excessive amount of job switching by the applicant.

Just recently, I was in the job search mode. I tried internet advertising. The first thing that happened is that my local newspaper had a job website that prompted responses. I also tried the national data-bases on line. I was pleased with the results that came from the newspaper because they were local candidates. I got very little, if any, response from the national boards and I wasted my money. Those sites may work better for different jobs and different localities and companies, but for me it was not worth it. Don't forget that when you use the internet you'll be getting resumes and responses via email. If your email box is already on overload, you may want to use just the faxes. On the up side, persons who respond to the ad via email are going to tend to be more technologically savvy.

After three days, you should have enough resumes to begin the screening process. Again, look for attitude. Look for the skills you need. I once got a resume from someone who listed their hobby as "watching television". That one got bounced from my list of potential interviewees. The resume should show that the person has made steady progress in improving their job skills and the scope of their responsibility. This speaks to attitude more than competence.

A few other tips on screening resumes include looking at the length of time an employee has held each job on the resume. There are some folks who switch jobs frequently. By this I mean a track record of more than five jobs in the last ten years. Or for an entry-level position, six months or less on a previous job is a poor indicator. If they've left other employers, they'll likely be a short-term match for your firm. Of course, look for the specific skills you need. Look for advancement. Someone who has been a payables clerk for the last fourteen years will not be a person that is interested in change or growth. That may be OK with you, just be aware of it. Match up the dates of education with the employment. This may clue you in to a person who has been in school at the same time they've held a job. This indicates a hard worker, and someone who perhaps took some initiative to advance their self by seeking outside education. Look for one page resumes. More than one page is a big issue. I feel that the person has an over-inflated sense of self to assume that I'm interested in more than one page.

If a cover letter is included, it will tell you a lot about attitude. The cover letter should be a short explanation of why they're applying and why you should consider them. I've had cover letters that state they're looking for a new job because they don't get along with their current boss. (No kidding!)

Narrow the field to five resumes, and then call to schedule an interview. Try to schedule all interviews on or close to the same day. Be prepared to interview during lunch hours or after hours, as some folks may need to come in during "off" hours from their current job.

Another mistake I see small business owners make very often is to hire a relative or a close friend. I've never seen this work out. The boundaries are not clear enough. Your business needs to be treated as a third person in the mix, a separate existence from yourself. You are its agent and protector. Your business's interests are not the same as the interests of your family members and friends, and therefore they will occasionally conflict. Your duty is to your business. Hopefully, you will make friends out of team members, but it rarely works the other way around.

CHAPTER VI – INTERVIEWING

The actual interview date is here. Hopefully you've scheduled all your candidates either on the same date or within the next day. If too much time goes by between interviews, you'll lose some objectivity and tend to be most impressed by the most recent candidate.

When interviewing the place to start is by remembering "HIRE ATTITUDE, TRAIN COMPENTENCE". Your first impression of the interviewee is going to mean a lot. In most cases, you'll be able to assess attitude right away. Look for professional dress (no jeans, low-cut blouses, short skirts, t-shirts, tank tops, flip-flops…). If the candidate is smart, they're putting their best foot forward for the interview, so it will be down hill from here on out if they become part of your team. Ask yourself if you can live with that.

I once had a candidate show up in jeans and a low-cut blouse which showed the tattoo just above her left breast. Her resume was really loaded with skills that I needed, but obviously, she was not the person I wanted greeting my clients in the front of my office. I shudder to think what she would have actually showed up for work in!

Take a pencil and paper in to the interview with you. Also bring in the job description and your interview questions that you've formulated ahead of time. There are some possible interview questions listed at the end of this book. Try to make them comfortable by offering them something to drink. Be prepared to do more listening than talking. After all, you should be pretty clear on what you want by this time. This is the time to find out about the possible team member.

At the minimum, you should get the following information about the candidate out of the interview: you should find out what caused them to respond to your ad. Discover what compensation they expect, along with the suitability of the hours and other benefits. Be sure to go over the job description in detail with them, asking them along the way if they understand the job as it has been described. If the interview is going well, tell the candidate that you'll train any part of the job; what you are more interested in is willingness.

The candidate will likely ask you to disclose how much the position is paying. Be prepared to give a range only. It is not until you've interviewed the last candidate that you will be able to decide on the exact salary. It is OK to tell them whatever benefits the firm offers.

If you like them pretty well at the end of the interview, take them around and introduce them to your other team members. You'll get valuable feedback from them about their impressions of the candidate, even if it is just for 30 seconds of contact.

Try not to offer the job on-the-spot to someone. Tell them you'll get back to them and try to have a date in mind that will be your decision date. Thank them for coming in and their interest in the job.

After narrowing down the field, check references. Call the references listed, and you'll get a better feel for the candidate and how well they will fit with your company. I've made the mistake of not calling references before, and hired someone who presented very well but was not a team player.

Always run a criminal background check on your candidates. Inform the candidate that you will be doing this, and get their permission. One in four businesses is victimized by fraud. Notice that they experience fraud, not that they are merely likely to experience fraud. Criminal background checks can be done online for a minimal cost. Statistics show that the dishonest employee is likely to be the most personable, willing person in the office. This means that they probably interviewed very well. Protect yourself at the outset.

CHAPTER VII – DETERMINE THE COMPENSATION

In chapter 3 you spent some time calculating the cost of the job. In this chapter you will rethink what you've calculated and integrate it with the information you got in the interview process.

What very likely happened is that you got a range of qualified candidates and there was an even wider range of salary. If you took the advice in the chapter about interviewing, you didn't make an offer at the point of the interview. So now you have a chance to really nail down what you'll pay your new employee.

I suggest making a worksheet that has a column for each candidate that was a possible fit for your business. Put their names at the top of the column, and then fill in the rows with qualities that are important. Here's an example.

	Wendy	Bud	Chloe	Steve
Attitude	3	3	3	3
Appearance	3	2	2	3
Length of time at prior jobs	1	3	2	1
Disposition	2	2	1	1
Communication Skills	2	1	2	1
Desired Compensation	3	1	2	1
Technical Skills	1	3	3	3

Here, the higher number is the more attractive candidate, and I used a scale of 1 – 3. A high number in desired compensation means that they are not asking for too much money. This is a good way to look at your candidates side by side. Can you guess who I would hire? I hired Wendy. While Bud, Chloe and Steve all had good attitudes, I didn't care for the way Bud and Chloe dressed, and Bud and Steve had poor communication skills. Also, they all wanted top of the pay scale. I opted for Wendy because she had attitude and a great demeanor, and since the job was for a receptionist, this was important.

The main idea is that once you've settled on the other things, you'll need to decide on the exact amount you'll start the new hire at.

Next comes the hard part. Open those purse strings!

Always offer health insurance. This will be the largest expense you'll have in connection with a new hire, and I'm not necessarily advising that you pay 100% of the cost. But if you don't offer it, you are begging to have the employee leave. If your new employee doesn't have coverage anywhere - and has no possibility of getting it from you - they will be constantly looking for it to be provided elsewhere. And they'll take a cut in pay to get it. The situation becomes even more dire if there are dependents involved. Ask your accountant about some tax leveraged opportunities available to small business employers with regard to health insurance. There are ways to make it work.

Don't expect people to work for low pay with a "commission" attached. And, don't count on making up for low pay with "bonuses". It's a fact that when people buy a new car, all they care about is the monthly payment. They'll buy a car that is within their monthly budget. The logic is the same with their paycheck. They want to know what their take home pay is going to be on a consistent basis. They want control over their lives, and can you really blame them? Remember, if they could tolerate a lot of volatility in their own paycheck or risk not being paid, they may well suited to become a small business owner rather than an employee...

Often, team members feel that commissions are out of their control. And to a certain extent, this is true. If they can't set price, or delivery terms, or modify the product, they really have a tough sell. I certainly don't advise giving them that degree of control over your product or service right away, meaning that at least initially they really will lack control. You've tied compensation to factors out of their hands. Unless they are strictly outside sales, try to pay a good salary rather than loading compensation toward commissions.

Bonuses are totally out of control. Recently, one of my clients gave his $15 per hour employee a $5,000 bonus. That's about 15% of annual compensation! Wow! She quit within the month. She used the bonus to set up her own competing business. Bonuses don't inspire loyalty. Neither do they inspire productivity, as they are completely at the subjective discretion of the employer. Start the new hire out with a good salary and pay smaller bonuses.

Consider offering retirement benefits. There are too many plans out there to be explained in detail here. But the basics are that there are ways to have a retirement plan in place that is inexpensive where you can elect to fund in good years and pass on tight years, and save taxes. Sometimes the taxes you'll save on funding for your employees may fund your retirement in full. This should be added to your list of things to talk to your accountant about.

Pay consistently. In other words, don't pay some people weekly, some monthly, some semi-monthly, etc. Put everyone on the same payday. Don't make things more complicated than they already are. One client I have pays one employee different rates depending upon which department of his business they guy worked in, and then adds commissions and overtime into the whole mix. Compliance is difficult enough without micromanaging pay scales and terms.

Be prepared at this point to also know when you'll be prepared to offer a raise and what will trigger that offer. This will be one of the first questions your new hire will want to know.

Be clear about little details at this point. After you make the offer, it will be too late to change terms. For example, will you pay mileage to your team member for errands or customer visits? Is there continuing education or a license required for the position? If so, will you pay it, or will the employee? Will you pay for them to go to school to improve their skills? Be very clear on which holidays you intend to close your business for, and whether or not to pay your team for some or all of these days. Be very clear about vacation days and sick days. If your employee has a sick child, will this count as a sick day? I live in South Carolina where everything closes for a little bit of snow. Will your office close? If so, when? And will you pay folks for this time, or do you expect them to make it up or take it as a vacation day? What about health insurance for dependents? Will you pay for unused vacation or will it carry over to the next year? If your salaried team member works lots of hours during heavy work load times, will you offer comp time? Get as much of this figured out as possible before you make an offer.

One more thing, be very careful about what you promise. Employees are very much like children. They remember every thing you've promised them. If you find yourself unable to deliver, it's much harder to take the promise back than to never have made it. I once heard an employee grumble that the business owner had promised him a bonus for keeping all the trucks and equipment clean. The trucks sparkled; the owner forgot his promise, and the team member quit.

Once you've figured all this out, it's time to make the offer to the employee you've selected.

CHAPTER VIII – EXTENDING THE OFFER

If you are at all like me, you don't advertise until you really need someone, and hopefully you've found a candidate that you are excited about. So you'll not want to wait to send a letter. You'll probably want to call them.

The first thing I'll suggest is to sound excited about having them come aboard. Say something like "I am so pleased to be able to offer you this job". Then go into the specific details, like compensation and hours and when you expect them to start. Answer any questions they might have about the position. Listen carefully to hear enthusiasm in their voice; you really do want someone who wants to work with you! Finish the call by telling them that they'll be getting a letter that will outline all that you've just told them.

Get the starting date clear. This is another reason why you might want to call the person in advance of writing to them. They've got things to take care of on their end. They'll need to give notice, work out the notice, and they may even want one or two days off before starting a new job where they'll need to be present consistently.

If you have other team members, this is the best time to communicate with them who you've hired and what their job duties will be, and when they'll start. This gets your team to "buy in" on the new person, so that there won't be any confusion over job descriptions or "turf". Remember, you're the boss, so don't ask them for too much feedback on what they think. This should be a meeting where you're telling them what you've decided and why.

Once the phone call is over, <u>write it all down</u>. I can't stress this too heavily. Write down everything you've just committed to over the phone. Go over all the decisions you made when you thought about compensation; such as holidays, comp time, retirement benefits, frequency of reviews, etc. I have done this with each person I've ever hired, and although it may feel formal and too strict, it will prove invaluable. Write this all down in the form of a letter to the candidate. Sign the letter, and provide a space for them to sign it and return to you. Also provide them with a return envelope (if you have other team members, be sure to mark it to your attention only, with "confidential" stamped on it).

Believe me; you'll need to refer back to this letter. Every single time I've had a team member leave, it has been necessary to pull out these letters. I've had folks want to be paid for comp time, for unused vacations, unused holidays, or they want retirement benefits that they're not entitled to. Don't neglect this step.

Include with your letter a W-4 for the new hire to fill out, and an I-9. These two forms are required to be maintained by the employer on behalf of the employee. Basically, the forms will report to you the employee's legal name, social security number, address and withholding requirements. Ask to get these forms signed and back to you with the letter that is formally extending the offer. If applicable, get health insurance enrollment forms signed and returned as well. I like to include one of our brochures with this package to encourage them to read about where they're coming to work.

When you get these forms back, start a permanent file for the employee. You're required to keep one, by law. Put their resume; the letter extending the offer in the file; the completed W-4 and I-9 in it. Also, I keep a copy of the job description, as it existed when this person started, in the file. This will help you keep track of what you told them the job would be and what progress they make over the term of their employment.

During the time between the extending of the offer and when the person reports to work, prepare their work area for them. Get them a desk, whatever office supplies you think they'll need, and a computer if they'll need one. Don't wait until they've started to take care of this, it will drag productivity down.

Place a copy of their job description on their desk, then you're ready for them to start!

CHAPTER IX – TRAIN! TRAIN! TRAIN!

The best thing you can do for both of you is to plan on being in the office for at least the first four hours of your new team member's first day. Clear your calendar, no kidding.

If you've hired someone conscientious, they'll probably be nervous their first day. Try to be there before they'll arrive. If you're feeling generous, bring in donuts or flowers for the office. These little touches will pay for themselves by providing a sense of relief for the new person, thus enhancing their capacity to be productive the first day.

The first thing to do is to take them around the office and introduce (or re-introduce) them to all your team. This avoids other team members peeking in, interrupting, or just gossip. Show them where the restroom is. Show them where office supplies are. If you have a kitchen, let them know what is available (if anything) to them without charge. Don't forget, they don't know if you'll even give them a cup of coffee! Then sit down with them and begin the day by going over their job description again.

At this point, an operations manual is invaluable. If you have one, give them a copy. Tell them what is in it, and tell them that they should check with the operations manual before coming to you to ask you about how things are done. Even the smartest person can't remember everything, especially if it is their first day and they are nervous. The operations manual will help them remember their training.

Starting with the job description will act as a trigger for all the things you want to train that day. Go through the whole routine. Don't assume they know anything. If they're not volunteering, with phrases like "I see" or "yes, I understand", then ask them! Don't be shy about asking "do you understand?", "Are you with me?" or "Is that clear to you?"

Another idea to help you with training is to delegate some of it to your staff. For example, if the job will involve answering phones, someone at your office might already be familiar with that. Have them train the new person. You might want to just go through the job description and write down the name of your other team member who can train them about that particular task. This way, not only will you free up your time, you'll also provide the name of someone they can check with if they get stuck, and they won't interrupt you. Try to train them on all the little stuff first (like how to use the copier or the fax machine). This may help prevent interruptions.

Ask them if they have all the supplies they need. If they have something that they're used to using in their job, you'll make their transition easier for them by providing it for them, provided it is immaterial to the way you conduct business. For example, I love a soft lead in my accounting pencils - it costs the same as regular lead, makes me more productive and loyal, and it costs nothing extra!

Have at least two tasks ready for them the first day that you expect them to be able to complete on their own on that first day. For example, if you're hiring a bookkeeper, save some bills to be paid for that first day. Make sure she can cut the check, get it signed, mark the invoice as paid, and file it properly by the end of the day. Hand as much work over to them as early as possible. It is pretty awkward for everyone when there is too much idle time during the first week. Introduce the full list of tasks once you've reviewed what they've already done.

I remember the first accounting job I had at a CPA firm. I was put in a room with a stack of files, and asked to do a "due diligence" on each of the entities in those files. I had no pencil, no paper, no idea what "due diligence" meant, nor any idea of what those business entities did. Someone ultimately helped me and I got the job done, but not without spinning my wheels for a while. In the end, I had to bug a partner more often that I like to remember.

The moral of that story is that time invested in training is time well spent. For every hour you neglect training, you'll loose two in errors, sub-par work, interruptions and questions, or just having the employee sit there, staring hopelessly at a computer screen. I understand you're busy. After all, you'd not have hired someone if you weren't really busy. I'm recommending spending the time training to ultimately *save* you time. This is the ultimate example of deferred gratification. Don't be tempted at this point to breathe a sigh of relief and say "phew! I found someone!" and then dump the work on their desk. Be patient and invest the time in clearly instructing and training the new team member. As an added bonus to proper training, your new employee may actually have some good ideas on how to get the job done in a more efficient way.

One thing I see occasionally is the **team member** who says, "I'd rather do it myself than train someone else to do it, especially since I'll wind up having to do it over anyway." This is totally unacceptable. It may be true the first or second time the task is at hand, but thereafter the time saved will pay off. Also, this type of attitude may be indicative of someone who is not a team player. Often these folks are superhuman, doing most of the office work themselves. The owner winds up being over dependent upon this one team member, the other team members feel left on the outside and resentful, and eventually the owner will be held up for more and more money as the "super worker" feels more and more pressure to perform and keep the balls juggled. So make it clear to all team members that you expect them to train and cross-train as many of the tasks of the business as possible.

Training never stops. Things change, employees leave, new technology makes old methods obsolete. As an employer, be prepared for never-ending training. In fact, make it part of regular monthly team meetings. Make it easy on yourself by asking one of your team members to train the rest of the team on how they do their job. Not only does this keep everyone trained, it brings the team member into accountability with their peers with regard to the performance of her job. It also provides a forum for one of your team members to look smart in front of the group, thus boosting morale. And lastly, you may discover misunderstandings that your employee might have about their job, providing an explanation for some mysteries.

CHAPTER X – THE IMPORTANCE OF FEEDBACK

The gist of this chapter is that no-one is a mind reader. Everyone needs clear, written instructions about what is expected of them, and they need to know how they are measuring up. They need feedback.

Most people have difficulty with confrontation. Feedback should never be confrontational. One thing I like to do is to visualize my business as a third person. Then I ask myself how well this third person (the business) was served by the team member. This keeps things from getting personal. I'm less likely to say something like "how could you possibly do something so stupid?" and more likely to say something like "gee that's too bad that the task didn't get done. That will be bad for revenue."

Another thing I like to do is to visualize the business as a sports event, like a football game. When a team player scores for my team, I usually stand up and cheer. I try to visualize my business as if it were in a competition, and to remember to stand up and cheer for folks who help the business score.

In general, there are two forms of feedback, formal and informal. Informal feedback is just casual conversation that provides the team member with some sense of how they're doing.

Let's begin with positive feedback. This is the most neglected form of feedback that I encounter. I can't count the number of times I've heard an employee say something to the effect that if things are going well they never hear a peep, but let something go wrong and there's hell to pay. Positive feedback is important. The most obvious form is to just say, "Great job." Here are some other suggestions: when I review a tax return, I almost always find something that needs to be corrected. The review of the return is written and stays in the file. I try to remember to write something positive at the end of the review for the team member. Some companies have jobs that are accounted for separately. In this case, once the final numbers are in, provide your supervisors and/or their team with the report showing the profit and some short praise. Team meetings are also a great venue for informal feedback. Just briefly mention the task, how the business was helped, and thank the team member in front of his peers.

Never speak about short comings in front of another team member. If you want to increase turnover, ruin a potentially great employee, and demoralize everyone in earshot, correct or humiliate someone in public. If another team member is party to your criticism, they know they'll be next, if they haven't already been publicly criticized behind their back. More people quit over being humiliated than for any other reason. It is the one thing most folks will not tolerate. I once had a partner who was a prime offender in this area. Although we had an otherwise fun workplace, paid well, provided flexibility, insurance and retirement, we had a revolving door of team members. If my partner was unhappy with someone's performance, everybody knew it. And public criticism generally only builds resentment rather than correcting the problem.

Next, be sure you've cooled off. I have a tendency to loose my temper or take things personally. Recently a team member really offended me. I had to wait three weeks to speak to her about it calmly. The payoff was that I was certain that I was in the right, and that my treatment of the team member was fair. Ultimately, the team member was asked to leave, but I have a wonderful sense of confidence that personal reasons did interfere with doing what was best for the business. And that is really the bottom line. In presenting negative feedback to the employee, keep the best interest of the business at the core. And remember, it's not personal. Again, it helps to regard your business as a separate entity from yourself. It will help you keep the best interest of the business first and foremost.

Some formal feedback is critical, usually in the form of written, formal evaluations. I rarely see any small business employer stick to this guideline. Put dates for annual reviews on your calendar and stick to them. Neglecting the reviews keeps team members in the dark about how they're doing.

You don't have to do them annually; you can do them more frequently. What I suggest is doing one at three months initially, then again after six more months have elapsed, and then again at eighteen months, or a year and a half after they start. Then move to annual reviews. Whatever you decide, let the employee know when to expect the reviews and then stick to it unless something fairly important comes up.

I don't like doing reviews. In fact, I loathe them. They are worse for me than for the team member. Here are some ideas on how to make them easier for everyone. First start with the written job description you used when you hired your team member. Create a checklist for it by simply adding a box to the right or left of the expected tasks. Then I go through the checklist and rate the employee on how they're doing, and I use a scale of 1 to 5, 5 being outstanding. On occasion I've also provided a copy of the blank checklist to the team member and asked them to rate themselves. Once you get the checklist back from the employee, compare it to your evaluation.

These checklists have several benefits. First, it reminds you both of the tasks that <u>are</u> being done well. This is important when there is someone who is doing some little thing that bugs you, but is an otherwise great team member. It highlights the areas where poor communication exists. This would be the case where the employee thinks they're doing something wonderfully, and you wish for a 100% improvement. It reminds you of things you thought should be covered but are in reality being neglected. Lastly, you have something objective, a written script if you will, to conduct the review objectively and impersonally.

Next contemplate whether or not you wish to offer a pay increase. Work out the numbers before hand. I never have a range, I always have a specific number in mind by the time the review is scheduled. Be prepared to inform them why you've given the raise (or not), and how you arrived at the amount. Let them know for how long this raise is effective. Will you raise it again in a year? six months? When?

Conduct the review in privacy. Close the door or do the review at a time when no one else is in the office. Don't take calls or interruptions during the review. Try to make them comfortable (they're probably really nervous) by opening with some small talk, neutral ground. Then proceed to cover the items on the checklist, reinforcing the good jobs being done, and talking about areas that could use some improvement.

Talk about the compensation after you've covered the list. Communicate the compensation in a way that lets the team member know that it is not really up for discussion or negotiable. Then ask if they have any other questions or concerns, and wind up with thanking them for all they do.

After the review, put it in writing. Summarize the key points, sign the letter and have the team member sign. Give them a copy and put your copy in the employee's permanent file, with the checklists.

Here is a mistake I made once. I asked team members to tell me how happy they were with their jobs and compensation on a scale of 1 to 10. I have worked hard to create the jobs that I wish I could have gotten when I was in the workforce. Of course, my team members rated me mediocre, and I thought I had done such an outstanding job in creating our work place! I was hurt and angry. On the bright side, some of my team members woke up to the benefits of working with me. I also eliminated a team member that was not happy and replaced them with someone who is delighted to be part of the team. But the realization that human nature is such that people will always see what they don't have rather than what they do have was hard for me to take. It brought out the "Scrooge" in me. The moral of the story is that team members rarely appreciate the job, just as a matter of human nature.

So remember the basics:

o   Don't neglect positive feedback

o   Conduct annual, formal, written reviews

o   Don't take anything personally

CHAPTER XI – "DANGLE THE CARROT"

Everyone needs hope. Some team members more than others. Some team members are quite content to stay within the job as it exists for years and years until they retire. If your business has such a position for them, great! More likely, your business will change and grow. If nothing more than technology changes it, your business will not be the same five years from now as it is today.

This chapter is about building a team that will change and grow with the business and a team that will stay. I call it "dangling the carrot".

The first thing to remember is that there really must be a "carrot." On a merry-go-round, folks don't grab an invisible brass ring. It really exists. The same must be true for whatever incentive you offer to inspire loyalty. It must be a real possibility of coming to fruition.

It might be easier to talk about what not to offer. Unless you intend to follow through, don't offer partnership or partial ownership. Don't offer compensation you can't afford. Don't offer a retirement plan you can't fund. Try to never reduce benefits.

In deciding what to offer it might be a good idea to start with the team member you really want to keep, and ask them what they hope to get from their career with you. Some may want the opportunity to work part-time. Some may want ownership. Some may want more money. The point is that offering someone more money who really wants to just go home early every day may not buy loyalty. So not all team members will be rabbits where a carrot would appeal, some might be cats, who would prefer fish.

Another suggestion in offering a good carrot is to think about what you wanted when you were an employee. When I worked in public accounting for other CPAs, what I wanted most was to have full client responsibility and work independently. This was promised to me, but never really handed over to me. I didn't want to be in business for myself, nor was I particularly interested in being a partner. I just wanted more control and more direct interaction with the clients. The CPA could have kept me a lot longer - and prevented me from being a competitor - by simply following through on a promise.

Once you have the particular carrot in mind, begin working on a plan to make it happen. Write target dates down for yourself and check your progress. Literally put the target dates on your calendar. This will help keep you from pushing the promise out into the future indefinitely. Don't communicate your time goals to your team member until you have a track record of reaching a couple of benchmarks. This will give you confidence in communicating the timeline to your team member.

For example, let's say I have a team member who wants to increase their pay by 20%. In order for me to promise this to him, I must first calculate the number that this represents. Then I need to evaluate how much I need to grow revenue in order to make this happen without taking a pay cut myself. Then I'll set revenue growth targets to mark the progress to the goal. After achieving the first couple of targets, I'll communicate with my team member that

I've remembered their desire, I have a plan to get there, and I think that I'll be able to get there in _ amount of time. This will buy a lot of loyalty and productivity.

On the other hand, my former partner and I had an associate that wanted to be a partner. We were both in agreement that this would be a great idea, but we failed to come up with a plan to implement this goal with even the smallest steps. We put it off, did not give a time frame, and ultimately lost a good team member.

Retirement plans and profit sharing plans are always attractive benefits. Before you offer these think about the proper plan that is right for your business; evaluate the cost and complexity of what you are offering. Be aware that some retirement plans must be funded every year, regardless of profits. Others offer the option of passing on retirement in less profitable years. Some can be as expensive as $10,000 per year to administrate. Some can be free. Always, always, consult your accountant before committing to a plan. Retirement plans are sold by a variety of sales people who get paid in a variety of ways, and they may not be selling you the product that is best for your business.

Be realistic about what you can offer. Ownership is the ultimate carrot. I currently have a client that lost a lawsuit involving a former team member who got the impression that partnership was offered. He lost the lawsuit and wound up paying a former employee a percentage of the value of his business due to misunderstandings about ownership issues. If you are OK with offering ownership do it formally, in writing, and commit yourself to the plan. When you consider this, consult an accountant for proper entity for taxation issues, and consult an attorney to protect yourself and your team member. Don't do this by yourself. You don't have to include the employee in these negotiations at first, just your counsel.

Also keep in mind that what you promise you can't take back. That is the surest way to drive someone out the door. So be sure you can really offer the carrot!

CHAPTER XII – WHAT DO I DO WHEN....?

This book does not guarantee that you'll never have bumps in your human resource road. Life is such that people quit, they get transferred, have personal difficulties, or it's just time for someone to go. This chapter will offer some suggestions to keep you on track.

SOMEONE QUITS.

This will inevitably happen. Human nature is such that the grass is always greener on the other side of the fence and someone will come along with what your employee perceives as a better offer. It may not actually BE a better offer, but your employee may see it as such. Again, it is human nature. And it's not possible to know everything your employee was thinking in reaching their decision to leave, so don't take it personally. For a small business owner, this is the hardest part – not to take the decision personally.

I've had folks quit for any number of reasons: a spousal transfer, mental illness, better offers. Once I even had someone quit to "teach us a lesson"! The employee felt undervalued and was certain we'd never be able to replace him.

Before they leave, try to get an exit interview. You can get a lot of useful information, and it may be the way you safeguard the business against loosing critical people in the future. Use the interview skills listed in this book to gain insight on why your employee is leaving.

Try to get something in writing as to why they're quitting. Ideally, they've submitted a letter of resignation. If not, draft a short memo stating your understanding of why they're leaving and have it signed. This will help you officially close their employee file, and it will prove invaluable in contesting any unemployment claims that may come about. I've seen employees quit job #1, and have job #2 not work out. So they quit job #2 and file for unemployment benefits from job #1.

At this point, it is critical that you've followed the steps in this book. If you've got your organization chart up-to-date, your operations manual is current, and your folks are trained, you will have very little trouble replacing an employee. If those things are not up-to-date, work on them before you hire. And, if your letter-of-offer is on file, this will guide you as to unused vacation, sick-time and overtime decisions you might face.

Try to regard it as an opportunity to re-evaluate where your business is and where it wants to go. This may provide you with an opportunity. For example, if you have two service providers doing very similar jobs, it might be a good time to promote the remaining one, give him a slight increase, and then hire someone that he'll train at a slightly lower rate. You may engender loyalty with your remaining employee, and you'll take a huge burden of training a new hire off yourself.

Or, it may be a chance to restructure your own workload. Again, move one of your remaining employees into a job that you've wanted to delegate and restructure their job into something entirely new.

Always remember to get their keys and any other business property they have in their possession. Don't trust them to get it back to you later. Even if you have to follow them home, get the stuff back.

Never allow more than two weeks notice. Even though you may feel that you need them to do the work, it is *always* to the detriment of the business to allow a person more than two weeks notice. It damages team morale when team members are facing a "short-timer" every day. This will be particularly true if the departing employee is leaving for a better opportunity. It is hard for the remaining team to keep focused on the good things about your workplace when someone else has decided that it isn't good enough for them. The exiting team member is likely to not perform their duties with the same degree of conscientiousness they had before they gave notice. And, if your feelings are hurt by the departure, the situation is ripe for an unpleasant explosion.

If your business is at all sensitive to competitor information trading or if you've concerns about security with regard to either physical assets (like a jewelry store) or your information systems (the person who quit is the administrator of your computers), get them off of the premises immediately. Two weeks severance pay is at your discretion, there are no laws to govern whether you must pay it. Even though you'll be put in a bind while trying to replace them, the risk is not worth it.

Whatever the reason they leave, be gracious. Let them know you're sorry they're leaving, even if you are having mixed feelings. You never know when you'll encounter the employee again and the reputation of your business is at stake. You'll boost your remaining team members' respect for you, and the respect of the departing employee.

Never re-hire an employee who has left to take another job. This never works out. After the employee returns, they begin to remember all the reasons they quit in the first place, and they become discontent, *again*. Also, in the back of your mind, you'll never trust them fully again. Additionally, it demoralizes the rest of your team. They feel unrewarded for their continued loyalty when they see an old employee fully re-instated.

PERSONAL TRADGEDIES STRIKE

Life is such that you or your employees may experience traumatic life events that will impact your place of business. Some examples are divorce, serious illness, immediate family members dying, or the onset of mental illness.

The employer gets put in a tight spot when faced with any of these concerns. The business needs that team member. If it didn't, you wouldn't have them on board. The employee may be a valuable employee that you don't want to lose, so it is in the best interest of the company to try to accommodate the team member. Turnover is costly, so there is an economic reason to try to work through the situation if possible. The circumstances can be so variable that the advice must be general.

The first thing to do is to assess how permanent this situation is going to be. If it is a serious, chronic illness this requires different considerations than a temporary set-back. The best way to assess this is to directly ask the employee how long they need special considerations.

Consider your options. Sometimes other employees feel motivated to help out, and will offer to pick up extra work for a limited period of time. The position might be one that could be restructured as a part-time position. You may be able to offer more time off now in exchange for more hours in the future. Or you may offer a leave-of-absence. Since you have a business to run, you may decide that the employee needs to be terminated.

Whatever you decide, communicate it to your team member and put it in writing. This will help you both remember the special considerations made to accommodate the team member.

EMPLOYEE GOSSIP STARTS

There is nothing that can bring more damage to the work place than a disgruntled, big-mouthed employee. Gossip, backbiting, denigrating the employer or the work place is an office disease that spreads like wildfire. And it costs real dollars in lost production, abuse of office facilities, and can even spread to your customers or clients.

The best medicine for this is prevention. Here are some ideas.

Keep team member compensation confidential. This is the most frequent reason employee gossip gets started. Whatever you have to do to keep it confidential, do it. Put a password on payroll functions in your accounting system. If your office is small enough, do payroll yourself. Keep payroll records in a locked file. Make it part of your operations manual that discussion of compensation among team members is grounds for immediate dismissal.

Hold regular team meetings. The more communication you have with your employees the less likely they are to communicate with each other and guess about what's going on in the office or why decisions were made.

Try to be open about change in the business. The more the owner is secretive about company policies, the more likely people are to form their own opinions and talk about them.

Once the office dirt starts flying, here are some ideas on how to stop it. Hold a team meeting and confront the matter head-on. Tell your team what you've heard and ask them about it. Don't name names about who said what, just state the idea of what you've heard. Tell them it needs to stop and why it needs to stop. The reason it needs to stop is that it creates negative energy in the office which can spread to customers. Negative energy also exhausts everyone needlessly. Tell them why their ideas are wrong. Make the confrontation in calm, even tones.

If the gossip still does not stop, find the main instigator and fire them. Then hold a team meeting and let your team know that you've let the person go. Tell them that you want an office of people who want to work with you and this was not a good fit. Explain it in a manner that lets your team know that you are acting in the best interest of all concerned.

I'M UNHAPPY WITH A TEAM MEMBER

No matter how careful you are, you'll occasionally make a mistake in who you hire. Or, the employees can change for a variety of reasons. Personal difficulties may impair their work habits, or they may develop bad habits after a period of time.

If you've followed the steps in this book, you are doing 90% of what you should do to keep an employee happy.

However, in order to protect your business, find out the reason why the employee is under-functioning. This is really going the extra mile and I truly hate this part of being an employer. But you need to know if *what you think* you're doing for your employees is really what you *are* doing for them. For example, one of my clients thought he was paying his team at the top of the pay scale. When we asked his team, they thought they could earn almost 50%

more at another job. The industry had changed and the employer had not kept current info on salary range. The reality, of course, was somewhere in between. Another one of my employers felt that he was offering compensation incentives for performance. The team felt they were being given a hopeless goal.

Before taking the time to find out what you need to know, make sure you're in the right frame of mind to discuss the situation with them. If they tell you why they're unhappy it is likely to either hurt your feelings or make you angry. Don't react, just put off any further discussion for at least a week.

Once you find out what is causing the employee to under-function, you can take the time to ask yourself if it is something you're willing to bend for. If not, then let them go. And, of course, try to document everything.

If you don't go through this process you may be setting yourself up for repeated turnover, or for second guessing yourself on the loss of an employee that had valuable potential.

Keep in mind that being unhappy with someone may not necessarily mean getting rid of them today. Think about your decision and give yourself time to make your mind up.

If you decide you can accommodate them in some way that improves the situation, clearly communicate with them the steps you are taking. Don't expect them to notice on their own.

I NEED TO FIRE SOMEONE

When I was a member of Results Accountants Systems, Ric Payne, one of the founders of RAS, gave me the following quote: "Use the FIFO system of managing employees". Ordinarily, FIFO stands for First In, First Out. However, when applied to human resource management, it means Fit In or F___ O___. It's a great quote. No matter what you do, you'll never please all your employees. And it is your business. Don't be afraid to let folks go. Everyone is replaceable and your business is so much better off when it has a team that is happy. So when someone just doesn't fit, let them go. If you've followed the steps in this book, you'll have no trouble replacing people with enthusiastic, happy team members.

Here are the steps for properly terminating someone, in order.

Prepare documentation on why you're letting them go. Write your concerns down and write your decision down. Make a copy of it for the employee.

Prepare a final paycheck. Have it ready to go and signed.

Invite the employee into your office or another private space and close the door.

In an even, non-accusatory tone, state that you have made a decision to terminate their employment. The reasons are documented in the memo you drafted. Go over the memo with them.

Ask for their office keys and any other business property they have in their possession (pager, laptop PC, etc.)

After they've returned their keys, give them their final paycheck.

Go with them to collect their personal belongings and then escort them to the door.

Meet with the rest of your team immediately. Inform them that so-and-so is no longer with the company and that the decision was reached in what you believe to be in the best interest of your business. Ask if there are any questions, but be prepared to answer the questions with "I'm sorry, I don't feel comfortable telling you that."

Go back to work!

CONCLUSION:

Human resource management is one of the most difficult challenges your business will ever face. Following the steps in this book will breed good habits for growth and stability within your business. Best of all, if you grow your business large enough, you can eventually delegate this, too!

CHAPTER XIII – EMPLOYMENT COMPLIANCE BASICS

Your first step in becoming an employer is to notify the federal government, your state government and possibly your local government that you intend to start having employees.

For the federal government, you must now get a federal employer identification number if you don't already have one. This done by filling out a form called an SS-4. It is a simple, one-page form. It specifically asks you if your business will be having employees. Be sure to answer these questions accurately. This will automatically prompt the IRS to send you appropriate forms and coupons for proper compliance. There are no fees due with this form.

If you've already got a federal employer identification number (EIN), all you need to do is get the proper forms to start payroll compliance. Your accountant will have these, or you can get them from your local IRS office.

For your state government, you'll need to register with them as an employer. Most states have a reciprocity agreement with the feds – meaning that they'll know if you've gotten a federal employer identification number and they'll ask you to register your business with them accordingly. Check out the website for your state tax agency to find the proper form to register with your state as an employer. There may be a fee for registering and getting the forms.

Next you'll need to set up an unemployment tax account with your state. Unemployment insurance is a program that is mandated by the federal government, but administered by the states. So you'll have an employer account with your state. Again, contact your accountant to help you find out how to set up an account or go to your state's website.

<u>The IRS</u>:

The federal government has publications that are available free. You can pick up some of these publications at your local branch of the Internal Revenue Service. Or, you can order them on line at www.irs.gov. There may be a shipping charge for these.

The beauty of an IRS publication is that whereas the Internal Revenue Code is written on an average reading level of grade 16, the publications are written in an average grade level 10. Simply put, they're easy to read. And because they are published by the Internal Revenue Service, they have the same authority as tax law. So if you're following the publications, you are complying with the law.

As an employer, you will automatically receive a "Circular E" every year. These publications include tax compliance explanations and new employer withholding tables.

Your state:

All fifty states have withholding requirements, except states with no state individual income tax. Those states are Nevada, Florida, Texas and Tennessee. You'll get information from your state automatically when you've registered with them.

<u>Payroll Services</u>:

Because payroll compliance can be so overwhelming, there are folks who make their living doing nothing but processing payrolls. The largest of these is ADP. Generally, they take the payroll information you give them about the employee (such as date of hire, pay rate, pay frequency, filing status, social security number, and address) and process all the payroll for you. They often offer perks for the employee such as direct deposit.

The advantage of these payroll services is that you get one bill for all payroll, and it includes all payroll taxes due plus the cost of the service. The service files all quarterly and annual forms for you and guarantees no penalties. They can process the payroll within two business days. And, as I mentioned, they usually offer direct deposit which is a really nice perk for both you (if you're salaried) and your employees.

The downside is that they are a big company. As such, you may not get the personal attention your account needs. I've seen them make errors, which has caused the customer great anxiety. They do require two business days to get the payroll out which may be a concern with regard to flexibility. Lastly, the cost runs about one to one and a half percent of the total payroll, so it can get expensive.

Leased Employees:

There are companies that take payroll compliance one step further. These are employee "leasing" companies. In this situation, the employee is technically an employee of the leasing company. The leasing company then bills you for the total cost of the employee, plus their fee. They work just like a payroll service in the sense that you choose the employee you want them to hire, they do all the payroll compliance and bill you one flat fee for the total cost. The added feature is that they often offer benefits that may be too costly for your business to provide on its own. For example, one of my clients switched to employee leasing because their employees then became eligible to obtain medical insurance as part of the leasing company's policy. This meant much lower health insurance premiums because my client was such a small group that their group policy was quite expensive. The leasing company, however, had a much larger pool of employees to spread risk over, hence lower insurance premiums. My client was also paying mileage to their employees for each trip to the office to pick up a paycheck. The leasing company added direct deposit to the features it was able to provide. The savings on medical insurance and mileage more than paid the leasing company's fee.

Generally, the employee leasing company will charge a 1½ % fee. With rising health and worker's compensation insurance costs, this may be a bargain.

Computerized Payroll:

In the event that you decide to try to do payroll yourself, get a computer program to help you with it. There are several good programs out there, specifically designed for small businesses. QuickBooks and Peachtree are both excellent small business accounting programs that have nice payroll features. You'll save the cost of the program in calculating payroll and accurately determining payroll deposits by avoiding penalties and detailed manual work.

Your accountant:

Payroll is very detailed and requires meticulous record keeping. Also, most of the required forms to be filed are now designed to be machine read. This means some investment in technology. Because employee leasing, payroll services and small business accounting programs have become so widely used, accountants have largely gone out of the payroll business. They just can't compete with the price and still make money.

However, a good local accountant (not one of the big firms) should be able to do payroll for your business at a reasonable cost when you have fewer than 10 employees. Once you get more than ten employees you'll either need an internal bookkeeper or a payroll service to take on this task. The reason the accountant should do it for you for fewer than 10 is because the compliance requirements are not as stringent for small employers, and they do it because they want your business to succeed. Of all the pitfalls a small business can encounter, payroll compliance is usually the area that trips them up. It is in the best interest of all parties to have the payroll done properly and a good accountant will help you with this.

What every accountant *can* do for you is to make sure you get registered properly, help you select the software program or payroll service you might need, or refer you to an employee leasing company. They can also review what's being done to assure that you are in good hands. If you've decided to do payroll yourself, they can help you file all quarterly and annual forms and/or provide you with blank forms you might need.

Remember, though, *there's no such thing as a cheap accountant.* There are services that are cheap, but they generally are poor accountants.

<u>Your labor board</u>

Every state has a labor board. The labor board enforces federal and state labor laws. These rules have to do with how to legally fire an employee, when you must pay overtime, when you don't have to pay overtime, etc. They can tell you what constitutes minimum wage and if that amount can be reduced for any on-site privileges you give your employees. For example, restaurants can provide a meal for their servers, and this reduces minimum wage for the estimated cost of the meal. Be sure you're clear about overtime and what you promise your employee. It is very common for a disgruntled employee to go to the labor board if they're terminated. Your labor board can send you, free of charge, a handbook to guide you in these concerns.

<u>General Payroll Compliance Requirements</u>:

Learn how to cut a payroll check. You should do this even if you plan to use a payroll service. You need to know how it works and to be able to explain it to your employee. See Appendix A for an example.

As an employer, you're required to pay over to the tax authorities the money that has been withheld from your employee's paychecks, plus your portion of the payroll tax expense. See Appendix B for this amount and how it is calculated.

There are strict, very stiff penalties for not paying over to the government the amounts that have been withheld in a timely manner. I have seen businesses fail for not properly respecting this rule. It is the most common trouble I see small businesses in. The reason the penalties are so stiff is that if the business has not given the IRS the money it has withheld from the employee's paycheck and the employee files a tax return claiming the amount withheld on their behalf, the IRS must give the employee credit for paying the tax – even though the IRS has not actually received the money. At which point the IRS becomes a lending agent, which they really don't like. So the penalties are very stiff, they start running within two days of a late payment, and they're hard to manage once they get started. The penalties alone can be 100% of the tax in certain circumstances. So don't be late!

The method by which you make these payments and the due date of the payments varies. Consult your tax advisor or call the Internal Revenue Service's general number, as to how to make the payments on time. Develop a system for yourself that will help you stay in compliance. Be sure you understand when the money is due and how to pay it.

The threat of these penalties is another advantage to using a payroll service, your accountant or an employee leasing company. If the payments are late – it's their fault!

Forms are required to be filed. Some of the forms are completely independent of payment requirements. The federal employer's quarterly report (form 941) reports on a quarterly basis to the IRS what your employees were paid and how much was withheld. The IRS then matches that to what you've paid. This is how the IRS knows whether or not to penalize you. They want the information quarterly so they can address employers who fail to comply in a more prompt manner.

You'll need to file monthly or quarterly with your state for income taxes and quarterly for state unemployment taxes. The unemployment taxes might be due with the actual return.

Annually, you must provide your employees and the federal government with W-2s, which show your employees' earnings, withholding and social security taxes. A copy of the W-2 also goes to the state. And you must report to the federal government the federal portion of the unemployment tax and what you've paid in state unemployment taxes.

The forms will be mailed to you, unless you're a very large employer. But don't wait for the forms; if you need blank ones get them from your accountant or the IRS. All forms are due within 30 days of the end of the quarter. The quarters run on the calendar, the first quarter ends March 31, etc.

Summary

This chapter shows why some small businesses avoid becoming an employer like they avoid the plague. Payroll is no fun. The cost of compliance is high since every paycheck requires tracking by date paid, employee, type of tax withheld, and unemployment liabilities. For each paycheck, there are at least ten details that must be tracked for each employee. Multiply that by two employees, paid twice monthly and that is 480 bits of data in one year to manage just two employees, excluding reporting requirements. Plus, this chapter has only scratched the surface. Other issues you'll face as you become larger may include retirement plans, dependent care benefits, cafeteria plans, medical spending accounts, tips, life insurance, and the list goes on and on. Be careful. Learn the basics of this chapter to be sure you have a general idea of compliance and then "choose your poison" – do it your self or outsource it!

CHAPTER XIV – RESOURCES

SAMPLE INTERVIEW QUESTIONS

What about our ad prompted you to send us your resume?

Tell me about the job you have now.

Tell me something you've done at your current job that you are really proud of.

Tell me about something at your current job that has caused you difficulty.

Tell me how you solved that difficulty.

What kinds of hobbies do you have?

Do you enjoy crossword puzzles or jigsaw puzzles?

What are your long-term goals?

If you could describe a perfect job for yourself, what would it look like?

What are your current job duties?

Which of those job duties do you enjoy most?

Which do you enjoy the least?

What do you think makes a team successful?

Have you ever been criticized at work?

What for?

How did you respond to this criticism?

What attributes do you have that you feel will benefit our business?

Describe for me what a balanced life for you would look like (meaning balance between work, family, recreation, etc.).

What do you feel would be your best contribution to our business?

What do you feel our business can provide you with?

What salary range are you looking for?

Why are you considering an employment change?

WORKSHEET FOR CALCULATING THE PAYROLL COSTS

Amount you'll pay hourly:

$ _____ x the number of hours per year _____ = $_____

Amount you'll pay as salary $_____

Amount you'll pay as commission $_____

Total Gross Pay   **$_____**

Add, Social Security Taxes   __X 1.0765__

Wages plus Social Security Taxes $_____

Add, Federal Unemp. Taxes($7,000 x .008)   __56.00__

Add, State Unemployment Taxes (call your accountant for this
amount) $_____

Add health insurance (monthly premium x 12) $_____

Add Workers Compensation insurance $_____

Add cell phone or pager $_____

Add any additional office supplies, rent, equipment $_____

Add retirement (if eligible and the plan is in place) $_____

Add computer costs (hardware, network access or programming,

   internet access, additional copies of software or network licenses)

                                                     $_____

Other costs $_____

TOTAL COST OF NEW HIRE $_____

APPENDIX A		
PAYROLL MECHANICS - THE PAYCHECK		
What it's called	The Dollar Value	Description/Definition
Gross Pay	$ 1,000.00	This is the pay you've agreed to pay your new employee. It can be a salaried amount or an hourly amount.
OASDI Tax, Employee share	(62.00)	This is the Old Age Security and Disability Insurance program that all wage earners must pay. The tax is 6.2% of every wage dollar earned up to a certain ceiling, which changes every year. The ceiling in 2004 is $87,900. The tax is mandatory, non-refundable.
Medicare Tax	(14.50)	This is the employees' share of Medicare Tax. The tax is 1.45% of all taxable wages. The tax is mandatory and non-refundable.

Federal Income Tax Withheld	(150.00)	This is the amount each employer is required to withhold from employee wages for anticipated federal income tax due. The amount is determined by the filing status of the employee, as reported to the employer on a form W-4 which is filled out at the beginning of employment. The IRS provides "look-up tables" to determine the exact amount to be withheld.
State Income Tax Withheld	(60.00)	This is the amount each employer is required to withhold from employee wages for anticipated state income tax due. The amount is determined by the filing status of the employee, as reported to the employer on the Federal form W-4. The state also provides "look-up tables" to determine the amount to be withheld.

Local Income Tax Withheld	(14.00)	Some localities, such as New York City, have required income taxes withheld just like the state. Consult your local tax advisor to learn if you are liable for this withholding.
Other Deductions	0	This might include an employee payment for family health insurance coverage, a retirement plan, an employee advance. Basically this can be a tool for the employer to use to ensure that he is paid for what the employee has committed to pay. Consult your tax advisor for the correct treatment of certain retirement benefits.
Net Pay	$ 699.50	This is the net sum of all gross pay and amounts withheld, and is the amount of the actual payment the employee receives.

The OASDI tax and the Medicare taxes are also called Social Security Taxes. These two taxes are paid one-half by the employee, and one-half by the employer. So the employer must "match" the tax.

Employers are, by law, required to be agents for the government. The government knows that tax burdens are such that the ordinary citizen can not be trusted to pay all their taxes by the due date. So the government has mandated that all employers act as an agent on behalf of the government to withhold from the employee's paycheck an amount that is estimated to be their tax liability. This means that the employer is responsible to pay over to the governmental authorities what has been withheld from each paycheck. These are called "Payroll Deposits". See the next page for how to calculate and pay these taxes.

As this illustration shows, the employer has contracted to pay the employee $1,000.00 for this pay period. However, the actual check to the employee is just $699.50. The difference of $300.50 is due to the federal, state and/or local governments. Consult your tax advisor or the IRS on how to pay this and when it's due.

Terms		Salaries and Wages	Social Security Taxes	
Definitions		**Gross Wages** - This is what you've agreed to pay your employee. Hourly or Salaried. Includes commissions, overtime, shift differentials, etc.	**OASDI** - This is the employee's contribution to the federal pension plan for the elderly or disabled.	**Medicare -** the tax contribution to the federal Medicare System
Rates		Determined by the employer	6.2% of all wages up to ~$90,000.	1.45% of all wages
Who Pays?	Employee		x	x
	Employer	x	x	x
Reporting Requirements		Annually, forms W-2 & W-3. Quarterly, forms 941 and state quarterly reports. Payment of taxes is independent of reporting. The amounts withheld from employee's checks must be paid on a regular basis to the IRS. Quarterly reports are filed to match payments with amounts due. Due dates of payment depend upon the amounts.		
Payment Requirements		As agreed upon by the employer and employee	Either by check payable to your bank together with a blue, pre-printed coupon, or by electronic transfer of funds. The total due is the total of federal income tax, plus **both** the employer's and the employee' share of the social security taxes. Due dates vary according to the amount.	

Terms		Federal Income Tax	State Income Tax	Unemployment Taxes	
Definitions		An estimated of the employee's federal income tax due based upon the information on the W-4. Tables calculate this amount based upon filing status and personal exemptions.	Same as the federal income tax withheld, except using state tables.	**FUTA** - Federally mandated program of benefits for persons who loose their jobs. Adminstered by the states.	**SUTA** - the state's tax for administering unemployment taxes and benefits.
Rates		Tables	Tables	.8% of the first $7,000 annual wages	Determined by state and experience.
Who Pays?	Employee	x	x		
	Employer			x	X

Reporting Requirements	Annually, forms W-2 & W-3. Quarterly, forms 941 and state quarterly reports. Payment of taxes is independent of reporting. The amounts withheld from employee's checks must be paid on a regular basis to the IRS. Quarterly reports are filed to match payments with amounts due. Due dates of payment depend upon the amounts.		Annual form 940. Payment is made quarterly once more than $100 is due. Payment is independent of reporting.	Quarterly, on forms that vary by state.
Payment Requirements	Together with the Social Security Taxes.	Same as the federal, but only state income tax amounts.	By check with coupon or by electronic draft quarterly.	Payment is due with the return.

About The Author

Lyn Richards is a CPA practicing in Columbia, South Carolina. She has over 20 years experience serving small businesses with accounting and small business consulting needs. She has been an adjunct professor at Midlands Technical College, and conducted local business development seminars. She is a member of RANONE, the leading global network of accountants devoted to delivering small business resources to accountants. She also runs her own small business "Business Builders". Her experience as a consultant and a small business owner has given her valuable insight on the struggles small business owners face in building their businesses into the dream they had when they decided to go into business for themselves.